You Just Can't Help It!

Your Guide to the Wild and Wacky World of Human Behavior

By Jeff Szpirglas

MAPLE
TREE

Maple Tree books are published by Owlkids Books Inc.
10 Lower Spadina Avenue, Suite 400, Toronto, Ontario M5V 2Z2
www.owlkids.com

Distributed in Canada by Raincoast Books
2440 Viking Way, Richmond, British Columbia V6V 1N2

Distributed in the United States by Publishers Group West
1700 Fourth Street, Berkeley, California 94710

Library and Archives Canada Cataloguing in Publication

Szpirglas, Jeff
       You just can't help it! : your guide to the wild and wacky world of
human behavior / Jeff Szpirglas ; Josh Holinaty, illustrator.

Includes index.
Issued also in an electronic format.
ISBN 978-1-926818-07-8 (bound).--ISBN 978-1-926818-08-5 (pbk.)

1. Human behavior--Juvenile literature. 2. Human biology--Juvenile literature.
I. Holinaty, Josh II. Title.

QP37.S997 2011   j599.9   C2010-904697-8

Library of Congress Control Number: 2010931642

E-book ISBN: 978-1-926818-15-3

Design: Clayton Hanmer   Cover Design: Barb Kelly

Canada Council   Conseil des Arts
for the Arts   du Canada

ONTARIO ARTS COUNCIL
CONSEIL DES ARTS DE L'ONTARIO

We acknowledge the financial support of the Canada Council for the Arts, the Ontario Arts Council,
the Government of Canada through the Canada Book Fund (CBF), and the Government of Ontario
through the Ontario Media Development Corporation's Book Initiative for our publishing activities.

Manufactured by WKT Co. Ltd.
Manufactured in Shenzhen, Guangdong, China in October 2010
Job #10CB2050

A   B   C   D   E   F

Owl kids

Publisher of Chirp, chickaDEE and OWL
www.owlkids.com

Contents

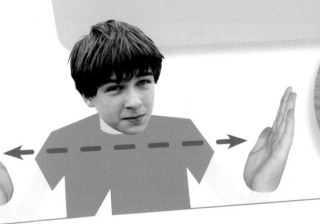

BELIEVE ME: YOU JUST CAN'T HELP IT!

Jeff

My name's Jeff, and I like weird things: horror films, reptiles, insects, teaching grade school—you name it! It probably helps that I *am* a weird thing. But so are you. And this book is all about why.

It all started when I was a kid. I was in the basement cleaning up when I found an old book called *The Naked Ape* by a guy named Desmond Morris. (No, there were no actual naked apes inside. Sorry.) Every once in a while, you come across something that changes your view of the world. *The Naked Ape* did that for me. Morris was a zoologist who decided to look at us—humans—and all our everyday behaviors, from the perspective of an animal researcher. I hadn't thought of it like that before.

Years later, when I was a teacher, it got me thinking that I've never seen a book like that for younger people. So I got inspired and decided to write a book on human behavior. Easier said than done! It meant a few years of scouring the Internet, afternoons spent thumbing through thick academic journals in dusty old libraries, and tracking down experts from around the globe by phone and email. I discovered that one of the best parts about writing a book like this is getting in touch with people whose job it is to do bizarre things, like sniffing smelly diapers or studying how a wave moves around a sporting arena.

Consider the result—this book—your official GUIDE TO YOU and all the WILD AND WACKY THINGS you do. It's about the science behind human behavior. The things we do as individuals (even the way you're sitting, right now, as you read this book) and as part of the society we live in (like how much space you feel comfortable with between you and a stranger) can be explained by science. You might think you're in control of everything you do, but after reading this book, I hope you'll think again.

But don't worry, it's not *all* science. I promise there will be some dumb jokes and goofy pictures, too. **I just couldn't help it. After all, I'm only human. And so are you. And being human is a pretty wild thing.**

SOUND

TASTE

TOUCH

SMELL

SIGHT

Chapter 1

SENSES SHOWDOWN

The world is a big, sometimes scary place. Good thing you're designed to make some sense of it using your (you guessed it!) senses. You know, those parts of you that receive and respond to what's happening around you. It's time to take a look at your senses in more detail, especially that famous five of touch, taste, sight, sound, and smell.

Right now, you're reading this book (I hope). Your sense of touch tells you that unlike a porcupine, it's safe to hold it in your hands. Your sense of sight reveals the letters, colors, and pictures. I suppose you could even find out what this book tastes like. But I don't recommend it.

Read on to discover what else your senses do. Just how do they help you interact with other people—for instance, by using eye contact in a conversation? And how do your senses keep you safe and healthy—by keeping you from eating spoiled food, for example, or from lying down for a nap on a roaring campfire? And of course, we'll answer that age-old dilemma: why should you not start a staring contest with a gorilla?

WHAT ARE YOU LOOKING AT?

You're using your sense of sight right now to read these words. Your eyes allow you to take in a lot of information about the world around you. Let's start with this page.

Pupil Power

Your pupils, the dark circles in the center of your eyes, will dilate (open) to let more light enter when you're in darker conditions. They'll constrict (get smaller) when it's too bright. Your pupils will also dilate when you're really interested in something. It's part of the automatic response your body has when you're excited. So check out your friend's eyes next time you're about to plunge down the track on a roller coaster.

Eye to Eye

You may not think much about eye contact when you're talking to someone, but scientists do. They've found that in most conversations, we give each other little looks, two or three seconds long. Looking eye to eye with someone shows understanding and interest, and also helps us to figure out whose turn it is to speak. Sometimes we look away from the person we're talking to, which helps us to understand what we're hearing, and to think of something, like a memory.

Stare-Down

Have you ever been told it's rude to stare? Other animals, like gorillas, which share many of our human facial expressions, don't usually stare either. A stare in the gorilla world is seen as a threat that could mean a challenge to fight.

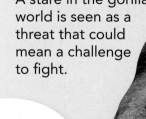

STARING CONTEST!

FACE-OFF!

You need only a half second to pick out a familiar face in a crowd. That's because humans can easily recognize the arrangement of eyes, mouth, and nose in a face. When looking at a face upside down, though, we have a more difficult time reading expressions. So what happens when scientists start to experiment with photos of faces? You guessed it: fun! A psychologist used a picture of a famous person, cut out the eyes and mouth, and flipped them around in the face. Then he turned the whole picture upside down. When looking at this picture upside down, it's hard to tell that anything's wrong. Until you turn it right way around again. Then the picture just looks freaky. Want to try?

Hi there. Don't I look handsome, even upside down?

TRY THIS

Still looking good, right? Now turn the book around so I'm right way up. Be warned: you might not like what you see.

You know that feeling when you sense you're being watched? Too long a look from another person can make you (or a gorilla) feel uncomfortable. That's what happened in one experiment, where a person sat on the sidewalk at a busy intersection and stared at drivers in the cars stopped at the red light. Drivers who noticed they were being stared at not only turned their eyes away, but often drove off more quickly when the light turned green. See ya!

LOOK OUT! WARNING:

This book, like most people, doesn't like to be stared at for too long. Are you brave enough to find out what happens if you keep your eyes on it? Don't say we didn't warn you...

Side effects of staring at book may include dizziness and blurred vision. In some rare cases, book will attack.

COLOR YOUR WORLD

Humans can see in three dimensions and in color. Most of us can make out around ten million different shades of color. But have you ever thought about how looking at certain colors makes you feel?

A Colorful Question

From sunrise to sunset—and into the night—we're surrounded by different colors. One theory about color says that the bright yellow and orange shades of daybreak energize our bodies, while the dark blue sky of dusk calms us down. Color and light reach us in waves. A warm color like orange has a longer wavelength, which according to the unproven theory, arouses us, increasing our ability to function in the day. And cooler colors like green have shorter wavelengths that relax us.

Howdy! I'm a YELLOW SQUARE! I'm totally exciting! Look at me. I'm yellow! How exciting is that?! See how many exclamation marks I'm using?!! You should go and do some jumping jacks! Do them now!!!

Hey. I'm a blue square. I'm totally cool. Chillax, dude. Okay?

Think PINK

A shade of pink known as Baker-Miller Pink has been tested for its calming effect. In England, holding cells for young offenders were painted in this pink so university professors could study whether the shade would calm the prisoners. And at Kinnick Stadium in Iowa City, the football coach had the visiting team's locker room painted pink. The coach hoped the color would put the other teams in a more relaxed mood, making them easier to defeat. The color did seem to have some effect—though not a calming one. Some visiting teams were so upset by the pink they lost their focus—and their games.

Be on the Red Team

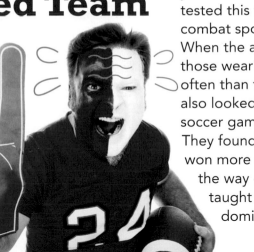

Does the color of your uniform affect your chance of winning? Researchers tested this theory by watching Olympic combat sports, like boxing and wrestling. When the athletes were evenly matched, those wearing red uniforms won more often than those in blue. Researchers also looked at the results of English soccer games over more than fifty years. They found that teams with red uniforms won more often than expected. Maybe the way our skin gets red in anger has taught us that red signals danger, dominance, or aggression.

GO, RED!

YES, this is a RED SQUARE!

Are you playing a competitive sport in the next few minutes? Do you need that extra edge? Simply point *You Just Can't Help It*'s distilled sample of 100% PURE RED at your opponent, and victory will be yours!*

*There is no guarantee that victory will be yours.

POISON DART FROG

When you see a yellow-and-black sign, you know it's there to warn of danger. The black-and-yellow bands on bees and wasps stand out in the same way. They're a signal that says: "Beware! I can hurt you!"

When animals' bright markings act as a warning, it is known as aposematic (ah-po-si-MA-tik) coloring. It can also be seen on poison dart frogs of Central and South America. These tropical frogs are so small they'd be hard to spot otherwise. They may look pretty, but don't touch. These amphibians secrete a toxin through their skin. There's enough poison in one type of frog to kill several adult humans.

Tasty Colors

Color affects more than just how we see things. The color of food also affects our senses of taste and smell. In one experiment, people said an orange-colored drink tasted like orange, when the flavor was actually cherry. In another experiment, making a drink a more intense red affected how sweet people reported that it tasted. Other studies have shown that the more brightly colored the food, the better people think it smells.

11

GET A WHIFF OF *THIS!*

You're totally immersed in a world rich with smells and tastes. Some of them are pleasant, but some of them are totally gross. And what you smell and taste can definitely make you act in interesting ways.

Your First Smells

Your nose developed after only fifteen weeks in your mother's womb. By twenty weeks, the nerves responsible for smell were growing. At birth, babies use smell to recognize their mothers, and it helps to forge a bond between baby and mom. Since human babies are so helpless, this strong bond is important for survival. Scientists know that other animal babies use their sense of smell, too. Blind baby mice, for instance, rely on smell to find their mothers' milk so they don't starve.

Stinky Snarl

When you smell something like rotting food or an unflushed toilet, your disgust reaction will likely register on your face. Your *levator labii superioris alaeque nasi*—one of your facial muscles—is responsible for the typical disgust expression. It narrows your nasal channels (so you breathe in less of what may be a toxic smell), wrinkles your nose, and curls your upper lip into a snarl that signals others not to come close. If the smell is coming from rancid food, the reaction helps to make sure you're not tempted to eat it, so you don't get sick.

sniff sniff

IOOO

The lining of a mouse's nose has around a thousand types of scent receptors.

450

A human's nose has only around four hundred and fifty types of scent receptors.

Disgusting!

The snarl you make when you're disgusted can also be set off by looking at gross pictures (of bleeding cuts or feces, for example). It can even be triggered by being in a situation you find unfair, such as being given different rules than someone else.

Savor the Flavor

If you had to choose between candy and vegetables, which would you choose? Most kids would opt for the candy. Even in the womb, you might have had a sweet tooth. Studies have shown that by fifteen to twenty weeks of age a developing human fetus gulps more fluid when there's noticeable sugar in it (and less when there's a sour substance present).

You have thousands of chemical receptors, called taste buds, on your tongue. While your tongue has only a few taste receptors for sweet, there are dozens that detect bitterness.

Smelling the Mood

Have you ever eaten enough garlic to make people in breathing range want to run away? A scientist went to a shopping mall to find out if good smells have the opposite effect. He and his team determined where nice-smelling parts of the mall were (like near the cinnamon bun store). Then they dropped pens or asked for change in different spots. They observed that shoppers were much more likely to stop and help in areas that smelled good. Another survey found that people's moods improved around "pleasant" odors.

Your senses of taste and smell are very closely related. Think of how hard it is to taste your food when you have a cold with a stuffed-up nose.

EXPERIMENT

Thirteen moms were asked to bring a fresh poopy diaper to the lab in a sealed bag to be part of a smell study.

QUESTION

Scientists in Australia wondered: *Do new moms prefer the smell of their own baby's poop to another kid's?*

OBSERVATION

You don't need an advanced science degree to know that poo doesn't smell nice. The way we react to poo—looking away in disgust, closing our nostrils—is a behavior that protects us from the harmful germs in feces. But scientists reasoned that since mothers of new babies were dealing with lots of icky stuff—vomit, urine, and feces—they'd have to get over their disgust.

STEP 1

Mom "A" puts her baby's diaper in a bag to bring to the science lab.

STEP 2

Scientist collects poopy diapers from Mom "A" and other moms, too.

STEP 3

Scientist places two diapers in identical plastic buckets with holes in the lids. One diaper is from Mom "A's" baby and one is from another baby.

STEP 4

Scientist closes the buckets.

Ahhh, the smell of science!

STEP 5
Mom "A" sniffs both buckets. Which is grosser?

STEP 6
Repeat experiment. This time, label the buckets.

STEP 7
Repeat experiment. This time, switch the labels on the buckets so they are labeled incorrectly.

WEEKS LATER

Remember to take diapers out of buckets!

RESULTS

Mothers tended to find their own baby's stinky diaper less gross than another baby's—both when the buckets weren't labeled and when they were correctly labeled.

SUMMARY

Why were moms more tolerant of their own baby's stink?

Perhaps by being around her own baby so much, each mom was just used to her baby's smells. Or a baby's poop might have hints of "relatedness" to Mom. If the poopy smell is familiar to the mom, does it seem less gross than the smells coming from "unrelated" poop?

HEAR THE NEWS

HEAR THE NEWS HEAR THE NEWS

Close your eyes for a minute (uh, after reading the rest of this sentence) and tune in to the sounds around you: your dad's voice, an annoying commercial jingle on TV, a lawn mower, the school bell.... Wherever you are, your ears pick up all the sounds around you.

HOW LOW Can You Go?

In a conversation, one person usually adjusts the tones of his or her voice, along with volume and pitch, in what researchers call *paralanguage*. These voice-tone adjustments can say a lot about who controls a conversation. People with less "power" tend to vary the frequencies of their voices more often, since they unknowingly try to match the frequencies of more dominant people. Try listening to a friend talking to the principal or an acquaintance he or she wants to impress. Does your friend's voice sound different when you're just casually chatting with each other in the schoolyard?

Cry, Baby!

Cute they may be, but when babies wail, it is not a soothing sound. Our ears are very responsive to dynamic, high-pitched noises that can change, like the wail of an ambulance siren. Some opera performers are able to use a technique called a singer's *formant*, which elevates their voices into a higher register, so they can be heard above an entire orchestra without a microphone. A newborn baby's cry is also able to reach the highest range of sound that a human ear can pick up. It's a survival technique built into the little ones. Since they can't look after themselves, their urgent cries ensure they'll get the attention they need, at any hour of the night or day.

Which Sound Is More Annoying?

a Crying baby
b Ambulance siren
c Opera singer

SHOP TO THE BEAT

Can music control your mind? Some stores and malls select background music they hope will help to boost sales. One researcher tested the effect that "fast" music (ninety-four or more beats per minute) and "slow" music (less than seventy-two beats per minute) had on shoppers. When the down-tempo tunes were played, shoppers moved more slowly than when there was no music, and much slower than when the fast songs were played. And average sales increased by more than thirty-eight percent with slow music. Seems the slowed-down music kept shoppers in the store longer, and they ended up buying more.

HOW TOUCHING

Touch is a powerful sense. It is used most by your skin (which is the body's largest organ). But other parts of your body—your tongue, your mouth, the inside of your nose—all use the sensation, too. Where would you be without your sense of touch?

Twice the Tickle

Back in the late 1800s, scientists identified two different kinds of tickling. *Knismesis* (niz-MEE-sis) is a light tickle, like the feeling of a feather being drawn across your arm. Many mammals demonstrate knismesis (like a horse fluttering its skin when a fly lands on it). Heavier tickling, known as *gargalesis* (garg-ah-LEE-sis), is the kind that causes laughter. It's only been observed in humans and some primates, like chimpanzees.

x2

Tickle: Good or *Bad*?

A good tickle can make you squeal with laughter. But sometimes the tickler just won't quit. Why can tickling feel both good and bad? One psychiatrist suggested that our most ticklish spots (the stomach, the sides of the torso) are located in parts of the body we'd want to protect in dangerous situations, like a fight, so maybe it keeps us aware.

TRY THIS!

One of our greatest thinkers, Aristotle, once asked an important question:

Why Can't YOU Tickle YOURSELF?

A good gargalesis tickle (the kind that makes you laugh) works only when someone else is tickling you. Part of the reason is that you need to be surprised. In experiments, people laughed harder when they were tickled with their eyes closed. Still think you can tickle yourself into a laugh attack? Go ahead, try!

ho ho!

ha ha!

hee hee!

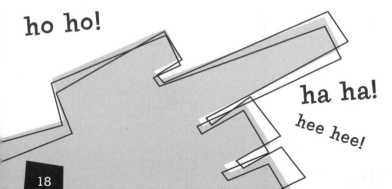

First Kisses?

Ever wondered how and why we started kissing? Some scientists have looked to the feeding behavior of birds for answers. Mothers often regurgitate food for young birds that can't leave the nest. Did our kissing begin the same way? In the prehistoric days before soft baby food, human mothers probably chewed food up for their babies and then passed it from their mouths to their babies' mouths. When babies started eating regular food, kissing may have developed between mother and child to show comfort or affection.

Kissy, Kissy

Is kissing good, bad, or totally gross? Nearly ninety percent of the world's population kisses, which means ten percent—or around 650 million people—don't. Before puckering up, check out these kissing stats:

The Good
- thirty lip muscles get a workout
- creates a bond between parents and kids

The Gross
- you're transferring saliva and mucus
- millions of bacteria may move from one person to another

The Unusual
- when kissing, nearly twice as many people turn their heads to the right as to the left

ARE YOU AN ANIMAL?
HOUSE CAT

Your uncle Charlie's mustache might look cool but can his facial hairs help him sense his environment? Not like a cat's whiskers can.

Cats have around twenty-four thick, flexible hairs on their faces. The bases of these whiskers are close to specialized nerve receptors, so they are sensitive enough to notice a change in the breeze. Cats learn that if they can fit their heads through a narrow spot without touching their whiskers, they can likely fit their whole bodies through. And since cats have poor close-up vision, their whiskers also help them hunt by feeling out their prey's movement and location when it's too close to see.

Chapter 2

IN A STATE

Think of all the different states and emotions you've experienced just over the past twenty-four hours. Did you have a dream-filled night? Did you bound out of bed or hide away under the covers when your alarm went off? Did you have a gigglefest with your friend? Did you feel a knot in your stomach before a big test?

The states and emotions you experience are important business. There are whole industries based around them, like happiness (from stand-up comics to sit-down sitcoms) and fear (roller coasters and terrifying films). It's not always easy to control these states—and some, like sleep, are just unavoidable.

Do you want to know more about the states and reactions your body goes through all day and night? The following pages might make you scream in fear. They might make you burst out laughing. They might even make you shed a tear. Hopefully they won't put you to sleep. Keep your eyes open and read on!

FEAR
THIS PAGE!

Does your heart race when you stand at the edge of a high diving board or up in front of your whole class? Fear is an emotion that causes a physical reaction. It's time to find out what fear looks like...

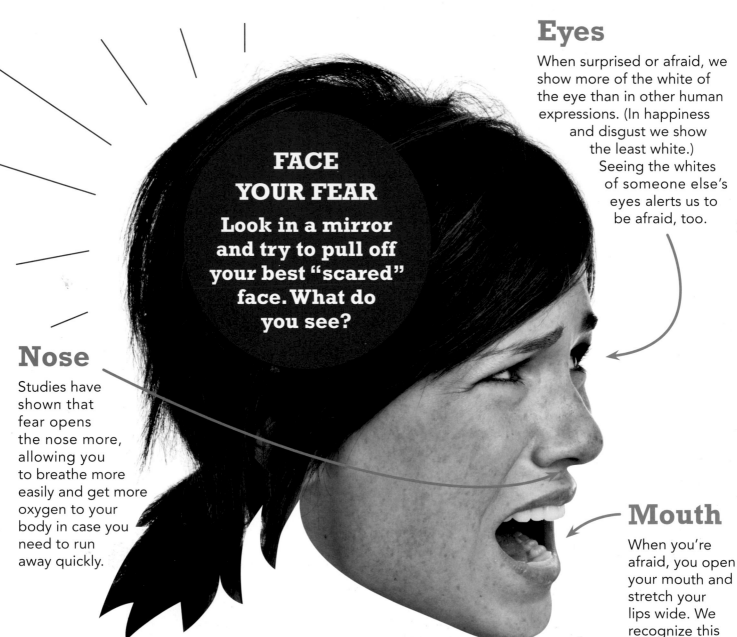

Eyes

When surprised or afraid, we show more of the white of the eye than in other human expressions. (In happiness and disgust we show the least white.) Seeing the whites of someone else's eyes alerts us to be afraid, too.

FACE YOUR FEAR

Look in a mirror and try to pull off your best "scared" face. What do you see?

Nose

Studies have shown that fear opens the nose more, allowing you to breathe more easily and get more oxygen to your body in case you need to run away quickly.

Mouth

When you're afraid, you open your mouth and stretch your lips wide. We recognize this as an expression of fear in others.

Seeing Fear

In one experiment, volunteers who simulated fearful faces were shown to have wider fields of vision. They could see more around them because their eyes were more wide open, and they were better able to scan back and forth. Being able to see what scares you might help you decide whether to face the fear or run away.

Instant Messaging

When you see something that scares you, a structure deep inside your brain called your amygdala helps you recognize danger. With help from another part of your brain— the hypothalamus—an alarm message goes out to all the parts of your body that react to a scary experience. And your brain's not wasting any time. How's a few thousandths of a second for instant messaging?

Stay or Go?

When you're freaked out, your body prepares to either stay and fight or run away (fast!). All animals have this built-in fight-or-flight response. Around thirty chemicals are released into your blood to make you super-alert. Your heart beats faster and your blood vessels dilate (get bigger) to send extra blood out to body parts like your brain and muscles. You might also feel like you're frozen in place. Your tense muscles are ready to fight or flee.

LAUGHTER
THE BEST MEDICINE?

HAA!

HAA!

HAA!

HAA!

Long before you could crawl, walk, or talk, you were able to laugh. Laughing isn't something you learn from your parents. It's something humans do automatically. And laughter works best when it's shared.

A Laugh Workout

Laughing isn't exactly like running a marathon, but a lot of research indicates that it's actually good for you. With a hearty laugh, you clear your air passages and relax any tense muscles. So go ahead, have a laugh workout today!

HAA!

HAA!

100=10?

One laugh expert has suggested that laughing one hundred to two hundred times in a day would give your body the same workout as rowing for ten minutes.

Laughing lowers your blood pressure, helps your blood flow, and improves how your heart muscle works.

Depending on how big your laugh is, you may use your leg, arm, and back muscles, too.

Your immune system, which keeps you healthy, gets a boost when you laugh.

Laughter, Pass It On

People are more likely to laugh when they hear others laughing. That's why TV sitcoms often use live studio audiences—so viewers at home can hear the audience's reaction and laugh along with them. But laughs can happen without a live audience, too. In 1950, TV viewers watching *The Hank McCune Show* heard the world's first pre-recorded laughing sounds, a.k.a. a "laugh track." This canned laughter came from a "Laff Box," which could be played like a piano to give off different kinds of laughs.

HAA! HAA!

DO-IT-YOURSELF EXPERIMENT

Can YOU Make Someone Laugh?

Turn to the person closest to you. Ask that person to laugh. If you get a funny look, just say you're doing a science experiment.

[WAIT AND SEE WHAT HAPPENS...]

Well? What happened? Did the person laugh? Was it convincing? A true laugh can't be forced. Laughing, like crying, is instinctive. Most people can't do a good job of laughing on command.

ARE YOU AN ANIMAL?
"LAUGHING" HYENA

Humans aren't the only species that laughs. Many primates, like chimpanzees and orangutans, also have been observed laughing.

However, if you happen to hit the Serengeti plains of Africa and hear a spotted hyena "laugh," it's not because some klutzy giraffe has slipped on a banana peel. That distinctive high-pitched sound means a hyena is seriously stressed out. It's likely being chased or attacked—usually by other hyenas trying to steal its food—and that's no joke.

25

ANOTHER DOSE OF LAUGHTER

HAA!

Still looking for laughs? You've come to the right place. Here's your handy guide to the language of laughter.

Pause , Before You Yuk-Yuk

Have you ever noticed that you don't—HA! HA! HA!—usually break into— HA! HA! HA!—laughter in the middle of—HA! HA! HA!—a sentence? Most laughter happens during pauses in speech where you would naturally use punctuation, like this comma, or this period. People who study laughter call this the *punctuation effect*.

A study looked at the punctuation effect in the conversations of deaf people using American Sign Language (ASL). Signers can laugh out loud at any point in a signed sentence. They're not using their vocal tracts, so they don't have to wait for a pause in speaking to laugh. Still, the signers laughed nearly three times more often during pauses in signing. So they looked for a natural break to laugh, too.

Looking for Laughs

One laughter researcher and his assistants went to public places like shopping malls and took notes on more than a thousand people talking and laughing. They found that most laughter came not after jokes but following normal comments people made, and that speakers laughed more often than listeners.

NOT FUNNY
A cream pie

FUNNY
Throwing a cream pie

JUST PLAIN HYSTERICAL
Your grandmother throwing a cream pie

Sounds Funny

When researchers analyzed recordings of laughter, they found that laughs sound similar no matter who is speaking. People make their laughs from short notes about 75 milliseconds long that get repeated every 210 milliseconds (about one-fifth of a second). The researchers also discovered that a "ha-ha-ha" laugh rarely gets mixed in with a "ho-ho-ho" laugh. Another researcher found that very few people actually made "ho-ho-ho" or "tee-hee-hee" sounds. Instead, she heard vowel sounds more like "har" and "oh."

TRY THIS!

Har-dee-har-har

How easy is it to make certain laugh sounds? Try some of the ones below and see which laughs sound natural and which ones we don't often make. Use the biggest voice you can.

(If your teacher or the librarian or anyone around you gives you a strange look, just tell them you're doing a science experiment. If that doesn't work, just keep laughing at them. Maybe your laughter will be contagious.)

hehoha hehohahoha haho HA haaha hooohaaa

He-he-he-he-he   Ho-ho-ho-ho

Ho-ha-he-ha-ho

Ha-ha-ha-ha-ha   Har-ho-oh-haha

Ho-ha-ho-ha, huh?

Cry Me a River

One of the first things you probably did coming into the world was open up your mouth and let out a good cry. Think you might shed a tear or two reading these sob stories? Well, if you do, please keep your leaky eyes off this page!

WARNING:

DO **NOT** CRY ON BOOK

WHAT'S IN A TEAR?

Water

Oils

Proteins

Manganese (mineral that affects mood when in excess)

Glucose (mmm, sugar!)

Salts (mmm, salty!)

Mucin (gel-like protein in your snot)

Urea (the stuff in your pee)

ESPECIALLY **NOT** HERE!

Weeping Brings Us Together

Your tears show other people how you're feeling, and so can ease a tense situation. Can crying actually bring people together? Let's say you get angry with someone and become so upset you start crying. Tears make your vision blurry and lower your defences—a signal that you need help. You are less likely to lash out at whoever made you angry. And when this person sees that you're crying, he or she will be more sympathetic to how you're feeling...hopefully.

TRY THIS!

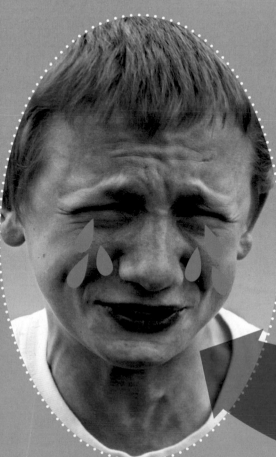

Erase Tears, Erase the Message

In one study, participants were asked to look at photos of crying faces. In some photos, the tears had been removed digitally. The participants found the faces in the photos sadder when they saw the tears. When the tears had been erased, some people read different expressions in the faces, like awe, concern, or confusion.

Block out the tears in this picture with your fingers. What emotion can you see now?

ARE YOU AN ANIMAL?
ALLIGATOR TEARS

Ever heard of someone crying "crocodile tears"? It's an expression that means you're pretending to be sad. Although there's no expression about crying "alligator tears," one alligator specialist decided to investigate if these close relatives of crocodiles do actually cry. The alligators he studied tended to tear up when they were eating food on dry land. It's unlikely the alligators were upset about that, so why cry?

The alligators might have produced tears to keep their eyes from drying out, just as we do. Tearing might also happen because of the huffing and hissing alligators do when eating. Air that comes in through the alligators' sinuses could push out liquid in the tear ducts, making it seem as if these reptiles are crying when really they're just having a good meal.

A REAL TEARJERKER

EXPERIMENT

Scientist William H. Frey II and his team of researchers asked volunteers to participate in a study to compare reflex and emotional tears.

QUESTION

Researcher and biochemist William H. Frey II asked: *Is there a difference between the types of tears we cry?*

OBSERVATION

Our eyes constantly make tears—around 1 mL (¼ teaspoon) per day. When our eyes react to something that irritates them, the tears we make are called reflex tears. We cry emotional tears when we're feeling sad, stressed, angry, even happy.

STAGE 1: REFLEX TEARS

To collect tears from something that would irritate the volunteers' eyes, the researchers chop up fresh onions in a blender.

STEP 1

Researcher puts the onions in a blender.

STEP 2

Researcher asks the volunteer to hold his head near the onion vapors for around three minutes.

STEP 3

Researcher collects the volunteer's tears in a test tube.

Hungry researcher makes French onion soup.

Good research makes me tear up!

STAGE 2: EMOTIONAL TEARS

The volunteers come back a week later. This time, the researchers show them sad movies: *The Champ*, *Brian's Song*, and the top tear jerker, *All Mine to Give*.

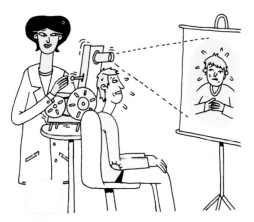

STEP 1

Researcher puts on a sad movie.

STEP 2

Volunteer gets emotional.

IT'S OK, IT WAS ONLY A MOVIE...

SOB

STEP 3

Volunteer collects his own tears (so he has privacy).

LATER THAT NIGHT

HA!

Volunteer watches his favorite comedy at home.

RESULTS

Volunteers made more tears from crying during a sad movie than when they were exposed to the onions. But the big difference came when comparing the content of the tears themselves. Reflex tears are ninety-eight percent water. Emotional tears have over twenty percent more protein in them than the reflex tears.

SUMMARY

All tears are not the same; something unique is happening when we cry emotional tears. Since crying, like exhaling or even going to the bathroom, is an exocrine (ex-oh-CREEN) process—a way of removing waste products or harmful materials from the body—perhaps we're literally crying out stress-related chemicals when we feel sad. This process helps our bodies get "back to normal" and relieve stress.

Time for Some Shut-Eye

Try as you might to stay awake, sooner or later your body will take over, and you'll feel the need to hit the hay for a good sleep. About one-third of your life is spent in sleep, drifting off in to some other world....

Counting Sleep

Eight hours of sleep a night adds up to fifty-six hours in a week, which makes nearly three thousand hours a year of sleep!

Why Sleep at All?

Sleep helps the body repair itself and conserve energy, and even helps you form memories.

Active Sleep

It might not seem like you're doing much when you're sleeping, but your brain never stops—it's moving in regular cycles all through the night. There are two types of sleep, rapid eye movement (REM) and non-rapid eye movement (NREM). In a good night's sleep, your brain goes through five stages of sleep (four NREM and one REM), about four or five times, shifting from NREM to REM about every hour and a half.

Counting Dreams

If dreaming mainly takes place in REM sleep (see right), and you do this around four to five times a night, that adds up to nearly two thousand dreams per year!

Know Your Sleep Stages

Stage 1

Light sleep. It's easy to be woken up in this stage. Your muscles can contract suddenly, as if you've been startled. Eye movements begin.

Stage 2

Your brain waves slow down, and your body temperature decreases.

Stage 3

Slow brain waves continue in the start of deep sleep. It will be difficult to wake you up now.

Stage 4

Ultimate deep sleep. You won't have eye movement or muscle activity. If you get woken up, you'll feel super-groggy.

Stage 5

In this REM stage, your eyes move around in different directions. You'll breathe rapidly and irregularly. Your limbs don't move. Your heart rate goes up. This is when most dreams take place.

Stinky Dreams

Does smell affect your dreams? A team of German researchers studied fifteen women to find out. Researchers hooked the women up to smell-making machines. Once the women entered REM sleep, the smell of roses or rotten eggs, or no smell at all, was piped into their nostrils. The women were woken up and asked about their dreams. Most women had pleasant dreams when smelling roses and unpleasant dreams when smelling rotten eggs.

Dream On

Experts disagree on exactly why we dream. What you experience in a dream might be taken from bits and pieces in your memory that you interpret as a story when you wake up, so dreaming might help with forming your memories. Others believe that dreams represent ideas or situations that help us try to interpret and solve problems in our everyday lives. So our brain keeps working away at our problems even while the rest of our body gets to take a break.

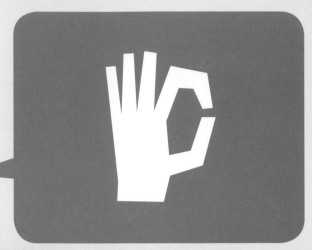

HUH?

What up?

;)

yo!

YEP!

BFF!?

:)

ttyl

um...

lol!

SAY WHAT?!

You can't help but communicate with people around you, whether you are speaking, signing, texting, or writing your words down. But communicating isn't just about using language. Your body sends out messages about how you think and feel, even when you might not want it to.

Sure, it might seem like you're in control of the language you use, but *what* you say and *how* you say it are tied so tightly together they're hard to separate. Think about it: can you keep your hands perfectly still when you're talking to somebody—even over the phone? Is it easy to look truly surprised when somebody ruins a "surprise" birthday party?

And what about those times when you decide to be sneaky and lie? Can you keep a straight face, or do you give away tiny clues that reveal the truth?

Whether or not you say a word, you're still saying an awful lot.

BODY TALK

How are you sitting right now? Are you slouched in your chair or sitting up straight? Are you turned away from other people or facing out into the room? Without saying a word, you're sending a message. Read on to see what else your body language can "say."

What are YOU lookin' at?

Arms Crossed

Folding your arms in front of your chest creates a barrier between you and other people, which could be a sign of disagreement, anger, or even stress. If you're in an argument, crossing your arms tells the other person that you're not willing to see his or her side. It can also be a self-comforting action (like giving yourself a hug), to relieve anxiety. Of course, it also depends on the person and the situation. Sometimes crossed arms just feel comfy!

Sticking Out Chest

Pulling back your shoulders, sticking out your chest, and locking your feet into place—like warriors, gladiators, or even modern-day professional wrestlers do—is a way to make yourself appear larger and more frightening. Standing taller and staring somebody down are other ways to intimidate, or make yourself feel more confident.

Shoulder Shrug

Hunch those shoulders, twist your hands so the palms are up, lower the corners of your mouth, and raise your eyebrows. Your body posture is totally submissive, and the shrug you've made shows that you're apologizing, uninterested, or even in disbelief.

WINK!
WINK!

I'M #1

UH, NO!

Didn't mean to...

Whatever

Hands Behind Back

When you hold your hands behind your back, you're totally exposing your torso and chest. This implies a lot of self-confidence. It's basically the opposite action of crossing your hands or arms in front of your chest.

Hands on Hips

This position signals that you're defiant or stubborn, and feel confident enough to show you mean business. Also, you're taking up more physical space than if your hands were resting at your sides. This projects your status as someone in charge. Add a tapping foot and you're saying you're impatient and frustrated, too.

NO JESTING about GESTURES

Shaking, pointing, gesturing: our hands are always on the move—and they have a lot to say.

Gestures at WORK

Whether you're speaking to your brother face to face or gabbing with a friend on the phone who can't even see you, your hands keep sending messages. Good thing, too. Research has shown that when you stop gesturing, it's harder to remember the words you want to say.

Talk *with* the Hand

Tell someone that you "caught a fish THIS big" and see if you can do it without making a gesture to show the size of the fish. Or try telling your friend about the amazing fireworks show you saw without pointing up. Gestures and hand signals are a part of how we talk. They help to communicate meaning, and provide the person we're speaking to with a visual for extra information.

Place left hand here

GESTURE-FREE ZONE

TRY THIS!

Think you can have a conversation without gesturing? Simply find a person to talk to, think of a really exciting topic, and then put your hands down in *You Just Can't Help It*'s patented "Gesture-Free Zone." Now keep your hands there while you talk—the whole time!

ga ga goo!

Getting to the POINT

Most babies start pointing before they can speak. It's a way of communicating without words. In one experiment, when shown something interesting, like a puppet, a baby would point—but only when there was another person there to see it. The babies did not point when they were alone. There was just no point.

Grabbing for Words

Gesturing helps others understand you, and also helps you literally "grasp" at your words and ideas when you talk. Let's say your teacher asks you to stand at the front of the class and tell your peers everything you know about lettuce. You know a lot about lettuce, right? But you'll be talking on the fly while thinking about what to say next. Hand gestures help you search for the words: round, leafy, crunchy—you name it. And gestures help smooth out the pauses while you take those ideas about lettuce and turn them into sentences. Maybe even salad.

SIGHT UNSEEN

People who have been blind from birth (so have never seen a gesture) use gestures as often as sighted people. Even similar types of gestures have been observed, such as making a C-shape to imitate pouring water from a container.

Conversation Starters for Shy Readers:

Some weather we're having...

Hey, is that a booger hanging from your nose?

Did I ever tell you about the time I _____?

Place right hand here

WHAT'S A YAWN SAY?

EXPERIMENT

Scientist Robert Provine figured that most people yawn when in a less interesting situation. He put his boredom theory to the test, using over thirty college students as guinea pigs.

QUESTION

Scientist Robert Provine wondered: *Why do we yawn, and what affects how often we yawn and how long a yawn lasts?*

OBSERVATION

It's hard to hide true feelings. Our body language gives us away. For example, it's not easy to stifle a yawn. There are many opinions about yawning, but not much evidence for why yawning happens.

STEP 1

Seat the volunteer behind a desk in a small, private room with a video screen.

STEP 2

Ask the volunteer to press a button on a box to record every yawn and how long it lasts.

STEP 3

Turn on rock music videos for thirty minutes.

STEP 4

Thank the volunteer and send her home, asking her to return another day.

This experiment is anything BUT boring!

STEP 5

The volunteer returns, but this time watches a thirty-minute video of a TV test bar pattern.

STEP 6

The scientist reminds the volunteer to press the button to record every yawn and how long it lasts.

STEP 7

The volunteer presses every time she yawns.

LATER THAT NIGHT

The volunteer rests her button-pressing finger.

RESULTS

On average, those watching the boring test bar pattern yawned nearly twice as often as those watching the music videos. Yawns lasted longer when people were watching test bars, too. Although males and females both yawned more when they saw the test bars, on average the males' yawns lasted around four seconds, while females yawned for three seconds.

SUMMARY

We yawn more often, and for longer periods of time, when exposed to something uninteresting. Yawning may help our bodies settle into another state, sort of like stretching as we get ready to relax.

41

THIS PAGE IS
HANDS-ON

Your hands are so expressive they have a language of their own, and can also signal different expressions in different cultures. Better brush up on your hand signals so you know what you're communicating.

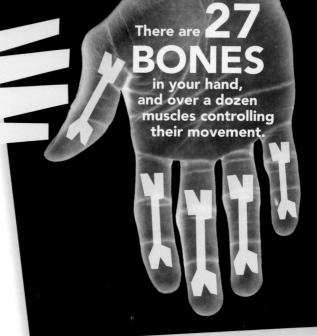

There are **27 BONES** in your hand, and over a dozen muscles controlling their movement.

O.K., Okay?

The letters "O.K." were first used by a Boston newspaper in the 1830s as a joke to mean "all correct." It soon caught on as a way to say that everything's all right. But the "O" can also stand for zero, something worthless. The circle also resembles the shape of a coin, and in Japan this symbol is used when asking for change.

V-Sign

The "V" has lots of history. There are legends about the V-sign that go way back, but it made a big impact when British Prime Minister Winston Churchill held up his two fingers as a "V" for victory in the Second World War. Later, in demonstrations against the Vietnam War and other wars, protesters adopted the "V" as a symbol for peace. And let's not forget the "V" of photography fame, when someone sticks two fingers behind somebody's head to give them rabbit ears.

Crossed Fingers

Want to make a wish? Or avoid bad luck? Or even go back on your own word? Crossing fingers started as a superstitious belief. One person would place an index finger over a friend's index finger in a cross shape to "seal" a wish. Over time, this turned into one person crossing his or her own fingers for good luck.

Hand of Rock

Shout "Rock on!" at a concert and you're sure to see the famous hand gesture: the middle and ring fingers are pulled down and covered by the thumb, leaving the index finger and pinky sticking up. The two pointy fingers look like a pair of horns. So how did this symbol get to be used by heavy metal rockers around the world? In the late 1970s, Black Sabbath band member Ronnie James Dio started flashing the sign to audiences, and it caught on. If you're wondering where Dio got the hand sign from in the first place, it was his Italian grandmother! She used the superstitious gesture to ward off the evil eye, a belief that bad thoughts or envy from another person could bring about harm.

Thumbs Up, Thumbs Down

When you give the thumbs-up symbol, you're usually saying something's good, and a thumbs-down sign means "bad." Hitchhikers use thumbs to find a free ride. Scuba divers use the thumb to signal it's time to swim back to the surface. The thumb-up is said to date back to gladiator fights in ancient Rome. When one gladiator was about to win, crowds (and the Roman emperor) would show their thumbs to signal the victor to make a final kill, or hide their thumbs to spare the other fighter's life.

The Nose Thumb

In one famous study, a group of researchers showed twenty famous gestures (including the others on this page) to over a thousand people in twenty-five different countries. Most gestures had several meanings, but the nose thumb had the most widely known one: to make fun of somebody else.

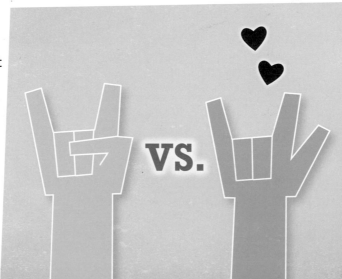

VS.

Watch those hands before you rock out. This rebellious symbol is one thumb away from sending out a completely different message. Just remove the thumb from the middle two fingers and stick it out to make the American Sign Language (ASL) sign for "I love you." But you're welcome to share the love, too.

LIAR, LIAR!

Everyone's stretched the truth at one time or another, but deceiving others isn't easy. Lying involves not only using your words but also mastering your body language. Most times, your non-verbal signals will give you away.

Pants on Fire

Okay, so your pants don't really catch fire, but your body will give out other clues when you are lying. You might start to sweat, your heartbeat increases, and your breathing might get deeper or shallower. Also, your gestures could get out of sync with your emotions. Saying you didn't see something happen when you really did and then waiting even a split second to shrug could be a big giveaway. These slips are called *deception clues*. When you lie, your mind has to not only think about the lie but also deal with how you feel about the truth. Sooner or later, a liar will "leak" a hidden emotion in a facial expression or an action.

Who stole the cookie from the cookie jar?

Uh...well, you see... erm...gulp.

avoiding eye contact

sweating

shallow breathing

increased heartbeat

laughing eyes

real laughter

The Eyes Don't Lie

Chances are you'll try to smile when telling a lie (and that's no lie). But if you're lying about how happy you are, it's the eyes that often give you away. A smile is one of the easiest facial expressions to make, but it's very hard to make a true smile if you're not feeling genuinely happy. A true smile involves certain muscles around the eyes. Only around two in ten people can voluntarily move the muscles surrounding the eye sockets, the outer *orbicularis oculi*, which give a pair of truly smiling eyes that distinctive "crinkly" look.

GOTCHA!

Look for this deception clue

Holding a smile for a long time probably means it's a fake smile. Most people who are smiling because they're actually happy hold their facial expressions for only around four or five seconds.

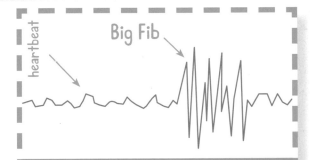

heartbeat

Big Fib

★ Detect-a-Lie ★

Police use a lie detector machine, or polygraph, to track body changes—like a change in heart rate—in a suspect during questioning. Some questions are irrelevant ones (for example, "Do you like balloons?"), used to make sure the machine is working and to see the normal readings for the person being interviewed. Others are "probable lie" questions (for example, "Did you steal those balloons?"). Polygraph results are helpful to investigators, but are not accepted as evidence of guilt by courts in many countries because they require interpretation.

TRY THIS!

Lying for Veggies

Go and tell whoever makes your dinner that you're dying for Brussels sprouts tonight. Try to be as convincing as you can be. Do they believe you? If you're lying, probably not. No matter how much you try to mask your disgust, you'll probably reveal your true feelings in a micro-expression—a quick flash of emotion that shows what you're really thinking. That grossed-out feeling might flash across your face for as little as one-tenth to one-fifteenth of a second. It might be fast enough to fool some people, but not all of them.

CAN WE TALK? :-)

WORDS—you use them all the time. Although we can communicate with only our hands and body language, we use a rich verbal and written language, too.

Fill 'Er Up

So, like, why do people, um, like, pause when they're talking and, uh, use words like "uh" and "um"? One study has suggested that we use a filler word, or *disfluency*, in every eleven or more seconds of speech. A disfluency like "um" might be used when the speaker is ready to talk but hasn't got the words out yet. Some researchers have even suggested that "um" indicates the speaker will use a long pause between words, while "uh" will signal a short one. So when you're getting up to give a speech in class, make sure you prepare beforehand to, uh, keep out your "uhs" and "ums," so, um, you're very clear about the message you're trying to, uh, give.

How Many Words?

When scientist Matthias Mehl wanted to see how many words people actually use, he developed the Electronically Activated Recorder. The EAR (get it?) is a tiny recording device that captures random sounds and talking. Over six years, and using nearly four hundred volunteers, Mehl's team went through hours of recorded conversations. They found that women on average used a total of

16,215 words a day, while
men used **15,669**.

That's a difference of only 546 words—close enough to say that men talk about as much as women. The big difference was between the least talkative person, who used only 695 words a day, and the most talkative person, who used around 47,016 words! Both, by the way, were men.

DISFLUENCIES YOU CAN USE

uh
er
um
like
I mean

DISFLUENCIES YOU CAN'T USE

sasquatch
ka-pow!
poopy pants

DISFLUENCIES YOU CAN USE TRAVELING

ben, euh (French)
eh, em (Hebrew)
eung, eo, ge (Korean)
øh, såå (Danish)
ya'ani (Arabic)

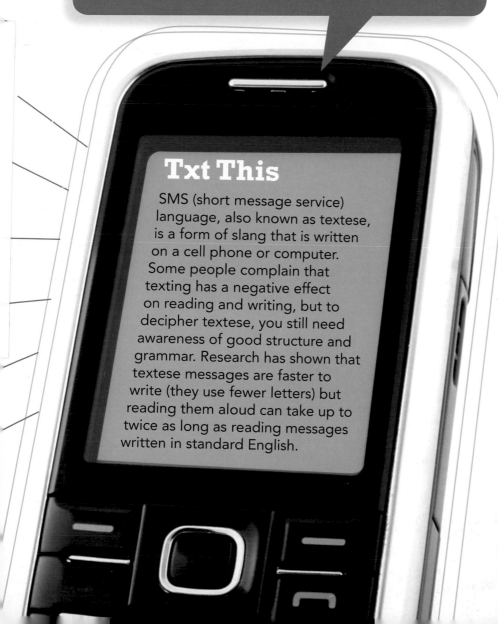

A Slang Thang

It's time to talk slang—words and expressions that mock "proper" language. Often, slang is coined by younger people who like wordplay, or by those who use words to show they belong to a certain group—like skateboarders. The word "slang" was first defined in *Webster's Dictionary* back in 1828 as "low, vulgar, unmeaning language." Clearly, Noah Webster didn't like slang terms mucking about with his giant book of words. But even if slang sounds improper, it does have meaning. Btw, what would Webster think of the words we're using today? Lol ;-)

Txt This

SMS (short message service) language, also known as textese, is a form of slang that is written on a cell phone or computer. Some people complain that texting has a negative effect on reading and writing, but to decipher textese, you still need awareness of good structure and grammar. Research has shown that textese messages are faster to write (they use fewer letters) but reading them aloud can take up to twice as long as reading messages written in standard English.

ARE YOU AN ANIMAL?

HONEYBEE

Animals don't use words, but they do communicate using ideas that can be strung together—much like words in a sentence. Even animals as small as bees have been documented creating messages using different "words." No, the bees aren't hanging around the hive chatting. Instead, they talk to one another using dance moves.

Bees use unique dances, like the waggle dance and the round dance, to communicate specific messages to their hive mates—like "Yummy nectar," "Wow! It's a long trip but it's worth it! I'll tell you where THE best food is," or "The food is close, but you have to follow me to get to it, suckers." Okay, so those aren't direct translations, but you get the idea.

Chapter 4

YOU + WORLD

If you're human (you are, right?), you need to live with other people. Whether you live in a small village or a bustling city, your life is full of relationships. Some are very close, like with your friends, and some are distant, like with a stranger you pass on the street.

How you act—and how you are treated—is affected by who you are in relation to others, starting with whether you're a boy or a girl, and your place in your own family.

It's not always easy getting along with everybody, having to share space in a classroom, a house, even at the dinner table. To get by when we're around others, humans have created a system of rules to make sure that nobody gets too stressed out. And with 6.5 billion people in the world and one packed planet, that's a good thing.

GØRLS & BOYS

You don't need this book to tell you that boys and girls are physically different. But what about behavior? Though most studies show there are many more similarities than differences, people who study gender do find some variation. Is any of this true for you?

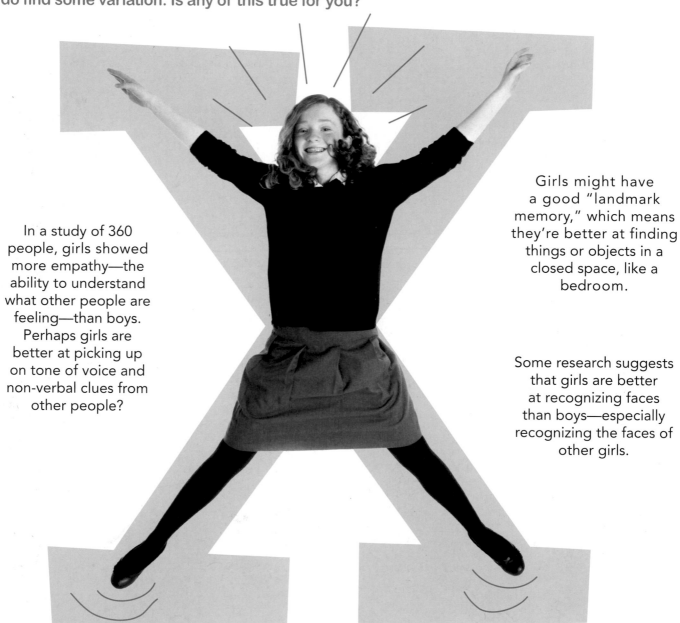

In a study of 360 people, girls showed more empathy—the ability to understand what other people are feeling—than boys. Perhaps girls are better at picking up on tone of voice and non-verbal clues from other people?

Girls might have a good "landmark memory," which means they're better at finding things or objects in a closed space, like a bedroom.

Some research suggests that girls are better at recognizing faces than boys—especially recognizing the faces of other girls.

Males do well at finding, or "disembedding," a simple picture in a more complex one.

Boys tend to have more spatial awareness than girls, making them good at reading maps or designing 3-D objects from pictures.

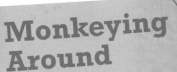

Boys might be strong systemizers—which means they're good at analyzing and exploring how things work, from a piano to a computer to an ecosystem, like a pond.

Monkeying Around

Why do girls play with "girl" toys and boys with "boy" toys? Is it because of the toys we're given by grown-ups? Does our society reinforce this? Or is there something else at work here? In one study, young vervet monkeys were given toys: a car, a doll, a stuffed dog, and a picture book. Male vervet monkeys tended to interact more with the ball or car, while more females were in contact with the doll. Males and females interacted equally with the book and stuffed dog. The scientist who conducted the study wondered if the idea of a "boy" or "girl" toy isn't just coming from our society. It may be that certain types of things appeal more to either males or females, possibly stretching far back to the days of early humans.

Why the X and Y?

The letters X and Y stand for chromosomes. Each cell of your body has twenty-three sets of two chromosomes, making a total of forty-six per cell. Your chromosomes determine everything from your hair and eye color to your gender. In girls, one of the pairs is the two XX chromosomes, and in boys, it's the XY pair. These two pairings are what makes a girl a girl and a boy a boy.

BRINGING IN SOME ORDER

Many things affect how you act, including your family members—the people you've spent your whole life with. Does the order of your birth predict how you act? Some researchers think so. Do you fit the personality profile?

First-Born

First words, first steps, first poop: the first child in a family gets lots of attention from the moment he or she arrives on the scene. Here are some characteristics often attributed to a first-born.

- eager to please parents, which means you're unlikely to rebel
- organized and conscientious
- good leader—after all, you probably take responsibility for your younger siblings
- don't have to share food with siblings (at first)

- the token babysitter in the family

DID YOU KNOW...

Even the first child to be born in a pair of twins can display some typical first-born character traits. One survey showed that most people elected to the United States Congress were first-borns.

Middle Child

Feeling stuck in the middle? Later-born kids, don't fret! You've got a special place in the family, too. There's nothing middling about your personality stats.

- parents are probably less worried about you, making you more relaxed
- you're probably the family peacekeeper: you've developed skills to get along well with others
- your friends are important to you

- because there's always someone older or younger than you, you may feel you never get your parents' full attention

DID YOU KNOW...

One study looked at the birth order of nearly three thousand scientists who were involved in big changes during the last four hundred years. The researcher discovered that twenty-three of twenty-eight scientific revolutions, like Darwin's theory of natural selection and Copernicus's discovery that the Earth orbits the Sun, were led by later-born children.

The Youngest

Sure, they call you "baby" brother or sister, even when you're, like, TEN. But being the youngest has its perks, too...

- you might be able to get away with things your older sibs couldn't
- you're probably the class clown; you'll do anything for a laugh
- you're not likely to give up when you don't get your way

- you'll get full parent attention when your siblings move out, but you'll have to wait for it
- you're less likely to win the same praise for your "firsts," like tying shoelaces or riding a bike, since your older sibs beat you to it

DID YOU KNOW...

Researchers found that later-born siblings were almost one and a half times more likely to try risk-taking or injury-causing sports, like hockey. And in a study of seven hundred brothers who played baseball, younger brothers were ten times more likely to steal bases than first-born brothers.

HAHA! I'M THE BEST!

Only Child

No brothers, no sisters—you're the star of the family. You might shine in the spotlight, but read on for more.

- spending time with grown-ups makes you act more mature
- you get one hundred percent parental attention
- no one to share food or toys with

- might be overly self-critical
- lots of pressure from parents (see one hundred percent parental attention above)
- might have to learn co-operative skills, like sharing, outside of the house

DID YOU KNOW...

In two surveys of nearly three hundred university students, which looked at what jobs they'd like to have, only children (and first-borns) were more interested in intellectual jobs, like office work or teaching careers. Later-born children preferred outdoor and artistic activities.

ARE YOU AN ANIMAL? CATTLE EGRET

If you think all this birth order stuff sounds unfair, be thankful you're not a later-born bird in a cattle egret family. These egret mothers lay their eggs over a few days, and begin incubating each as soon as it is laid. That means the early-laid eggs hatch first and get the first go at the food provided by their parents, leaving less for the younger ones.

But things could be worse if you're an animal like an ant, shark, or wasp. In order to compete, older siblings of these species sometimes actually EAT their younger siblings. Yeesh!

SPACED OUT

Where are you sitting reading this book? In your bedroom? Or a crowded public library? You probably don't think about it much, but the amount of space around you affects your behavior.

What's Your Zone?

When two different animals get close, say a lion and an antelope, there's a certain amount of space the prey animal (in this case the antelope) will feel comfortable with before it runs away…or the predator animal (the lion) attacks. This is called *flight distance*. Animals of the same species that live together, like a flock of birds, don't generally run—or fly— for their lives when they get close to each other. But you can't help but feel uncomfortable when a human stranger stands so close you're touching. Scientist Edward Hall measured distances between people and how it affected their behavior. He classified our personal space in zones.

ZONE 1:
Intimate Distance
(touching to 45 cm/18 in.)

Standing this close—almost face to face—with a loved one will feel okay, but with a stranger it will feel uncomfortable and crowded. At this range, you can definitely smell the other person and feel his or her body heat. Chances are you'll speak in a low voice or a whisper.

Please don't shout.

ZONE 2:
Personal Distance
(45 cm/18 in. to 1.2 m/4 ft.)

Personal distance is the space people would put between themselves to shake hands or talk to a friend at recess. People speak at a normal volume at this range, and body heat isn't detected. But if you haven't brushed your teeth, the other person might smell it.

ZONE 4:
Public Distance
(3.7 m/12 ft. or more)

As people move farther away from each other, it becomes harder to see certain details, like eye color. An important public figure like a world leader or member of royalty keeps a wider distance apart from others. When giving a speech, a public figure will raise his or her voice and speak in an exaggerated manner.

ZONE 3:
Social Distance
(1.2 m/4 ft. to 3.7 m/12 ft.)

Social distance is the space people normally put between themselves, in an orthodontist's waiting room, for example. When talking to somebody, it helps to keep eye contact to let the other person know you're listening. Voices get raised the farther apart people get.

The Official
You Just Can't Help It! Personal Space Invasion Game

How do people feel when their personal space is invaded? Play to find out!

You'll Need
- a copy of this book (awesome, you've already got one!)
- a willing volunteer (friends work best)
- some space (don't try this in a closet)

How to Play
1. Stretch your arms out in front of you like a zombie. Get your partner to do the same.
2. Stand far enough apart that your fingertips are touching. Bravo! You've created Personal Space.
3. Now stand close enough together that only the width of this book fits between you. You've created Intimate Space!
4. Keep standing and keep staring. Who will be the first to get uncomfortable and leave? You or your partner? The last person standing WINS!

Too Close to Look

The next time you're crowded into a busy elevator, look around. Are strangers staring at the numbers for the floors rather than at each other? Once people's space gets invaded, especially by strangers, they might tighten their lips and look away or close their eyes more to avoid making eye contact.

CROWD CONTROL

How do you feel when strangers crowd you in a line? Some crowds get along great—like those at theaters and arenas—but some can drive you nuts. When your space is invaded, you might not be able to control your own reactions.

Wait in Line

Does it feel like you're always lining up with a crowd for something—the bus, the gym, the movie theater? In the world of waiting, there are two kinds of lineups: multiple lines each leading to a single person (like at a fast-food restaurant) or one big, snaking line that leads to several servers (like at the bank). Although the snaking line is bigger, most people prefer it—because these lines work on a first come, first served basis. With several smaller lineups, there's always the frustration of watching someone get ahead of you and get served faster.

PARK THIS!

Parking lots can be crowded spaces. Two researchers studied hundreds of drivers in busy shopping mall parking lots to see how people react to being crowded. They even sent in cars to crowd drivers trying to leave their parking spots. They found that when another driver was waiting for a spot, the person leaving took an extra seven seconds on average to pull out. When the waiting drivers honked their horns, the person leaving slowed down by another twelve seconds. Why the delay? It's possible that when drivers notice another car trying to take their spot, they get more cautious. Or maybe they become protective of the territory of the parking spot, even if that doesn't make sense.

HOW BIG IS YOUR SOCIAL CIRCLE?

You may spend a lot of time in crowds, but how many people do you have a close personal relationship with—your friends, family, and peers? We normally keep in personal contact with lots of people, although adults tend to stop at around 150 people. Teenagers are more comfy with around seventy to eighty people.

A Brush with...Butts?

Have you ever been in a store looking at something to buy when someone bumps into you accidentally? If so, you've experienced the "butt-brush" effect. Huh? Researchers reviewing video footage noticed that shoppers at a necktie rack positioned near the door of a store were getting bumped by people entering and leaving. The more they got bumped, the more likely the shoppers were to leave the tie rack—without buying a tie. When the researchers told the president of the store, he moved the tie rack away from the main entrance. The result? Fewer butts were "brushed" and more ties were sold.

toot!
/|\

Gross!

ARMY ANT

We've all been stuck in a car in a traffic jam. It's no fun. Humans should take a lesson from army ants to keep things moving along.

Raiding colonies of army ants move in groups of up to 200,000, in trails as long as a football field. That's a lot of ants to keep organized! So what's their secret? The ants lay down trails of chemicals, which tell following ants to stay in lanes and to keep moving fast. The ants will even make bridges with their bodies for other ants to use if there are any potholes in the way! It's one thing when all the ants are moving in the same direction, but once they turn back with their food, returning ants take up a center lane. The fast-moving outgoing ants take two outside lanes and just keep things flowing.

GIVE A WAVE

EXPERIMENT

Scientists studied video recordings of waves in stadiums that held over fifty thousand fans. They examined the movement of people in a wave and how waves start.

QUESTION

Scientists from the University of Budapest in Hungary asked, *What does it take for a huge crowd of people to work together and cooperate quickly?*

OBSERVATION

When thousands of fans at a sporting event unite and create a wave—a group of fans stands up together and raises their arms in the air, then sits down, while the fans in the next section carry on with the motion, and so on—it's an amazing example of a large crowd working together effortlessly.

HOW AN AUDIENCE WAVE WORKS

FIG. 1

Inactive phase (sitting down).

GO, TEAM!!!

FIG. 2

Active phase (moving up).

FIG. 3

Refracter phase (back into sitting position).

RESULTS

The scientists realized that the audience is acting like an "excitable medium," a group of individual units that can pass along signals to other members in a "wave," and nobody needs to direct them. In a huge crowd, it takes several fans next to each other to stand up at the same time to trigger the wave and start the active phase.

SUMMARY

A wave happens only when the audience is sitting and getting excited. Fans can't be totally focused on the game, or there's no wave. They can't be too bored, either. A good wave typically needs about thirty people to start it, especially in a big stadium that can hold fifty thousand people. Once started, a wave will usually go clockwise around a stadium at about twenty seats per second. As people gradually get less excited about keeping the wave up, there's a relatively short breakdown of the cycle and the wave will stop.

59

GOING OUT IN PUBLIC

Congratulations! You've nearly made it to the end of the book. By now you're no doubt feeling in control of your actions, right? Think you're ready to brave the big wide world out there? How you behave depends on where you are. Ready to play by the rules?

At the Table

Table manners: there seem to be endless rules for how you sit at the table, which utensils to use, and when to leave. We've had them for years. People even write books about the stuff. One of the most well-known early books on manners was written by Erasmus of Rotterdam in 1530 and called *On Civility in Children*. Hugely popular in its time, it offers advice that might be out of place today. For instance, if you started chewing a piece of food too big to swallow, Erasmus suggested you quietly turn around and toss the piece away. He also suggested compressing your belly to keep from breaking wind at the table. Good to know.

Not so loud!

After you.

Use your fork.

Excuse me.

Don't slurp!

SIT UP STRAIGHT!

Don't chew with your mouth open!

Say please and thank you!

Clapping: YES or NO?

Going out to see a live show means that you're probably going to be expected to show your appreciation at some point. When the curtain falls at the end of a play and the actors come out to take a bow, you'll look rude if you don't start clapping. The thing about clapping is that it depends on what you're seeing. A group of heavy metal rock stars would be upset if you weren't hooting and hollering and raising your fist during the show. But if you tried that at a classical concert, you'd get kicked out! Silence is required until the end of the whole symphony to give respect to the musicians. Use the handy guide (right) to brush up on all the rules of concert behavior you might need to know.

Swear on It #@!*

Swear words are only words, but they can offend. Usually we swear when we want to speak with emotion or get a reaction. Swearing has been compared to the way we use car horns: it can be used for joy or surprise, but usually it's for expressing anger. Research shows that two-thirds of all swearing in the English language has to do with frustration or anger. And why do we consider using it to be "bad" manners? It's possible that this dates back to England in the seventeenth century, when groups of people who wanted to change manners formed the idea that bad language was for people who were less educated, meaning that if you wanted to move up in the world, you didn't use certain words. Darn!

What to Do at a CONCERT: The Basics

Classical Concert

- Stay seated
- Dress up fancy
- Don't hum with the music
- Don't clap between movements
- Turn your cell phone off

Rock Concert

- Stand up, punch the air with your fist
- Torn jeans and leather look cool
- Scream the words as loud as you can
- Go nuts between each song
- Use the light of your cell phone to wave during ballads

MIND YOUR MANNERS

Why do we think of "good" and "bad" manners? It's something we need to learn, and something your parents probably like to remind you about. Manners are funny. Depending on where you live in the world, some normally "bad" behavior—like belching after a meal—might even be considered polite. The trick is to know how to behave properly in a situation. Manners allow people to feel secure in groups and social settings, like in school, a movie, or a restaurant. If we all know what is expected and we play by the rules, our behavior won't upset others, and we won't feel stress trying to figure out how to behave in every new situation. And that makes us all feel good.

Here we are. It's the end of the book.
Well, almost.

So what do you think? Are you really in control of the things you do? Or are you some wild, crazy animal who just can't help it?

That's not for me to say. I know where I stand.

What about you?

Index

Also available by Jeff Szpirglas

GROSS UNIVERSE
Your Guide to All Disgusting Things Under the Sun
Illustrated by Michael Cho

"This book will be irresistible to the very same middle schoolers who regularly resist science...highly recommended." — NSTA RECOMMENDS

2007 YALSA, Popular Paperbacks for Young Adults
2005 Independent Publishers' Award,
    Juvenile & YA Non-fiction Category, Finalist
2005 Canadian Children's Book Centre,
    Our Choice Starred Selection
2004 Canadian Science Writers' Association,
    Science in Society Award, Finalist
2004 Resource Links, Best of the Year

THEY DID WHAT?!
Your Guide to Weird & Wacky Things People Do
Illustrated by Dave Whamond

"Children who read this book will look at history and science with new enthusiasm and curiosity, and teachers will be able to demonstrate that history is not as boring as some may think." — SCHOOL LIBRARY JOURNAL

2007 Ontario Library Association,
    Silver Birch Award, Honour Book
2007 Canadian Toy Testing Council, Recommended Books
2006 Atlantic Library Association,
    Hackmatack Children's Choice Award, Finalist

FEAR THIS BOOK
*Your Guide to Fright, Horror,
& Things That Go Bump in the Night*
Illustrated by Ramón Pérez

"Szpirglas is a veritable expert at goosebumps."
— SCHOOL LIBRARY JOURNAL

2009 British Columbia Library Association,
    Red Cedar Book Award, Finalist
2008 Ontario Library Association,
    Silver Birch Award, Honour Book
2008 Atlantic Library Association,
    Hackmatack Children's Choice Book Award, Finalist
2007 Canadian Children's Book Centre,
    Our Choice Selection

JUST A MINUTE!
A Crazy Adventure in Time
Illustrated by Stephen MacEachern

"The key here lies in relating time to everyday events, and Just a Minute! is packed with examples that young readers will understand and enjoy." — QUILL & QUIRE

Acknowledgments

Writing a book like this means consulting a number of other sources: books, magazines, journals, and the Internet. Equally important are the experts in their fields who have helped check the facts in the book.

Put your hands together for a big round of applause for the following: Gerianne M. Alexander, Ph.D., Texas A&M University; Thomas R. Alley, Ph.D., Clemson University; Adam K. Anderson, Ph.D., Department of Psychology, University of Toronto; Barbara Annis, author *Leadership & the Sexes*; Jo-Anne Bachorowski, Ph.D., Vanderbilt University; Robert A. Baron, Ph.D., Spears Professor of Entrepreneurship, Oklahoma State University; Tavis J. Basford, MD; Donald W. Black, MD, University of Iowa; Trevor Case, Ph.D., Macquarie University; Hanah Chapman, Affect and Cognition Laboratory, University of Toronto; Jeanne F. Duffy, Ph.D., Harvard Medical School; Robin Dunbar, Ph.D., University of Oxford; Andrew J. Elliot, Ph.D., University of Rochester; Karen Emmorey, Ph.D., San Diego State University; Professor Jay Fisher, Yale University; Jim Fisher, Ph.D., Edinboro University of Pennsylvania; Jean E. Fox Tree, Ph.D., University of California, Santa Cruz; Fabia Franco, Ph.D., Middlesex University (London, UK); Mark G. Frank, Ph.D., University at Buffalo, State University of New York; Nigel Franks, Ph.D., University of Bristol; William H. Frey II, Director of the Alzheimer's Research Center at Regions Hospital in St. Paul, MN; Carol Kinsey Goman, author *The Nonverbal Advantage*; Paul Greenbaum, Ph.D., University of South Florida; Stanford W. Gregory, Jr, Ph.D., Kent State University; Phillip Haddy, University of Iowa Hawkeyes; Christine Harris, Ph.D., University of California, San Diego; Oren Hasson, Ph.D., Tel Aviv, Israel; Peter Hepper, Ph.D., Queen's University, Belfast; Russell A. Hill, Ph.D., Durham University; Wendy L. Hill, Ph.D., Lafayette College; Kay E. Holekamp, Ph.D., Michigan State University; Timothy Jay, Ph.D., Massachusetts College of Liberal Arts; Nenagh Kemp, Ph.D., University of Tasmania; Eric Kramer, Ph.D., Bard College at Simon's Rock; Richard Larson, Ph.D., Massachusetts Institute of Technology; Frederick T.L. Leong, Ph.D., Michigan State University; Professor Tony McEnery, Lancaster University; Matthias R. Mehl, Ph.D., University of Arizona; Ronald E. Milliman, Ph.D., Western Kentucky University; Nick Neave, Ph.D., Northumbria University; Robert Provine, Ph.D., University of Maryland, Baltimore County; Barry Ruback, Ph.D., Pennsylvania State University; Graeme Ruxton, Ph.D., University of Glasgow; Danielle Saint-Onge, Wife; Joel F. Sherzer, Ph.D., University of Texas at Austin; Charles Spence, Ph.D., University of Oxford; H. Dieter Steklis, Ph.D., University of Arizona; Boris A. Stuck, MD, University Hospital Mannheim; Frank J. Sulloway, Ph.D., University of California, Berkeley; Joshua M. Susskind, Affect and Cognition Laboratory, University of Toronto; Nan M. Sussman, Ph.D., College of Staten Island, CUNY; Kent A. Vliet, Ph.D., University of Florida. And a big thanks to my extraordinary editors, Maria Birmingham and Anne Shone.

All photos royalty-free (iStockphoto, Dreamstime, Photolibrary, Shutterstock) except page 57 (army ant): John Mason / Ardea.com.